Winter

Kaya Leslie

BookLeaf Publishing

India | USA | UK

Winter © 2022 Kaya Leslie

All rights reserved.

No part of this publication may be reproduced, stored in a retrieval system, or transmitted, in any form or by any means, electronic, mechanical, photocopying, recording or otherwise, without the prior written permission of the presenters.

Kaya Leslie asserts the moral right to be identified as author of this work.

Presentation by *BookLeaf Publishing*

Web: www.bookleafpub.com

E-mail: info@bookleafpub.com

ISBN : 9789357449151

First edition 2022

DEDICATION

To the readers, the writers, and the wandering souls.

You are every precious thing.

To the women in my life that showed me what love is.

To you, K for everything.

ACKNOWLEDGEMENT

Thank you to the beautiful beings that helped me discover that seasons are ever-changing.

PREFACE

'love me when i'm winter

when I don't know how to love myself'

when hurt talks

when hurt talks,
it says unfair things
spitting little pieces of itself
like shards of glass into the palms of your hands
the bottom of your feet
it wants you to hurt
the way it hurts.
that way,
we are not cruel
and

    alone.

bones

I am under construction
renovations in the main room
landscaping memories of what was,

life is always redecorating a place I'd like to call
home.
searching for contractors to come tell me, touch
me, show me
where my home is, to help me mold it- shape it
-build it

and

it always crumbles.

forclosure to a god I know exists not in the sky
or in the way he says I love you
but somewhere deep in the bones of my
foundation

losing my religion

I am the sum of my experiences
these words on the page like a prayer I keep
telling myself.

'everything is ok'

but-

the longer I sit here writing,
missing you feels like losing myself

and-

I know you are not coming to find me.

home

love is setting a place at the table for someone
who is never coming home.

love is leaving parts of yourself with someone
else and hoping they'll come back to you

love is the most painful thing we have to endure

but-

maybe one day he will find me

and love can embody what it has always meant
to be;

home

find me

It's time to let it in
give myself time
and
        space

to move through all of the bruises/now faded

still tender/ that overtake me

some in more intimate places than others

some in places I'm afraid to go,
unsure if I start falling down this path
that

I
  will
      be
         able
             to
                come

back to you

goodbye

In the beginning, it was slow
you warned me this could hurt
that -you- would hurt me
and I told you
I wasn't scared
that being hurt by you
is my choice
-but-
you didn't have to do it you know-
follow through on
the only word that holds any meaning to you

-goodbye-

love letters

you are unable to end our story

you are scared to leave me here alone,
in the middle of this thing we call life

its this thing I call darkness.
It reaches up from the earth, hands reaching for
my soul
and-

I'm tired

you can see it in my eyes
the defeat

its a reflection of your love
your presence in my life
like a light that's burnt out

and yet
you can't seem to end our story
stuck living in an epilogue
what our lives could have been

I've been holding on so hard

to something only I want to exist
and you-

still can't close the book.

but I'll do it for you
set you free, my words left running with you in
the wind
the connotation behind my eyes
like an ocean of all of the love letters you wrote
to me

I didn't know my story would end
in tragedy
I didn't think you'd edit yourself out of my life
but here we are
and-

this chapter has everything to do with the
nothing you left me

seasons

I spend a lot of time chasing the sun.

sometimes it's him, the warm brown of his eyes,
or the freckles on his cheeks.

sometimes it's the way light reflects off water,
little reminders of what heaven is like

I somehow think that happiness can only be
found on the sunny days
with laughter, love and warmth.

and-

maybe that's my problem

no one ever told me winter can be beautiful too.

mirror

have you ever looked at yourself
and realized that you haven't become
what you always thought you would?
that who you wanted to be

is
not

in fact

who you ended up with.

slow-burning

the thing about a love like ours is that it never
really disappears. it may just be a
slow-burning wick, always lit- warm, but alone.
It lights the dark with soft memories of laughter,
intimacy, of the very essence of you and I-
but then maybe it would be you.   and.
I.
not you and I
not in the way I want it to be.

yes, our light is stronger together. when we are
in the same room it's as if the sun has arrived,
reflections through your eyes, the lightness of
my laugh, the love between our hands

but there is only one candle.

I worry that my will to keep warm, to keep
burning, to keep loving you is stronger than your
will stay.

but-

I know you've figured out I'll love you anyway.

scars

the scars of his freedom
leave my chest exposed

his words ripped through my rib cage
echoed inside of my lungs
and I can't breath

don't bring tomorrow
because I already know
what you'll say
a quick
'yep, you too'

and our story
is not a love story-
its a story of what could have been
had we wanted the same things

someone's nothing

what is it like to be someone's everything ?

I catch glimpses of light in the eyes of my
partners,

but my reflection looks too dim.

and easily, I become someone's nothing

its funny though, because I thought it would
come as a surprise to feel like nothing

but at the end of the day nothing is the only
consistent I have

and-

there's comfort in loneliness because if no one
cares

no one can you let down

sinking

I wonder how many times I am going to end up
back here
sinking
watching my soul being passed around the room
handled by men who do not understand
what it is to love a woman like me
whose heart is more than on her sleeve
too delicate to be picked up
to muddied to touch
too damaged to be held

the worse part is,
I have been held before
felt love that touched beneath my bones
that held the very essence tenderness

but

here I am,

sinking.

leave me in the cold

winter just wasn't my season

fall reminds me of you

our relationship was like summer and when life
got back to normal -september rolled around and
you left

it wasnt even fall and you left
the storm that followed seemed hard to weather
but
then I realized that I dont need you

that I am so much more than the words you said
about me
that maybe you dont even know me

and yet

the days where its cold in the morning and the
sun shines, my heart sings and when I dance its
always about you

and I look for you
and I look for you

and you're gone-

then rain comes and it comes and it comes and it
comes

but

I fucking love winter without you.

walk away

I owe no apology for doing what is it that I do to
repair the parts of me that you broke when you
decided that walking away was easier than
loving me

when you decided that maybe someone else's
bed is just a little warmer, their laugh not as
loud, their hips curving just enough to reel you
into what you desire most-

anyone who isn't me.

everything

I am everything I hated about you
I hurt people the way you hurt me

maybe when you walked away
you took all of my beauty

and I embodied all of our pain.

red flags

empty is hollow
overwhelm is a space that never stops moving
safety doesn't exist within the walls of my mind
red flags litter my soul

I understand why he walked away,

if I had the choice, I would leave me too.

big unmovable things

big unmovable things
like the spaces between

you
    and
I

this space takes all of what
I want to hold
and moves it

just
    out
        of
           reach

love me when I'm winter

love me when I'm winter

when my toes are cold
and I forgot my sweater

love me when I forget what sunshine feels like
when my eyes don't come up from the ground

love me because I can be spring
wait for me as I grow into my soul
watch me as I dance in the stars

love me when I'm lost
when my feet can't touch the earth
and I can't quite find the words to say I am my
own universe

love me when I'm quiet
when I'm stuck between everything autumn
and I can't quite figure it out

love me when I'm winter

when I don't know how to love myself.

snow storm

if I could be anything

I think I would be winter anyway-

I want to be the aftermath of a snowstorm;

breathtaking

strong

peaceful

free

winter breaks you open

in order to set you free